First Facts™

Health Matters

Food Allergies

by Jason Glaser

Consultant:
James R. Hubbard, MD
Fellow in the American Academy of Pediatrics
Iowa Medical Society
West Des Moines, Iowa

Capstone
press®

Mankato, Minnesota

First Facts is published by Capstone Press,
151 Good Counsel Drive, P.O. Box 669, Mankato, Minnesota 56002.
www.capstonepress.com

Library of Congress Cataloging-in-Publication Data
Glaser, Jason.
   Food allergies / by Jason Glaser.
   p. cm.—(First facts. Health matters)
   Summary: "Describes food allergies, how they are diagnosed and treated, and
how to prevent allergic reactions"—Provided by publisher.
   Includes bibliographical references and index.
   ISBN-13: 978-0-7368-6391-9 (hardcover)
   ISBN-10: 0-7368-6391-5 (hardcover)
   1. Food allergy in children—Juvenile literature. I. Title. II. Series.
 RJ386.5.G553 2007
 618.92'975—dc22   2006002817

Editorial Credits:
Shari Joffe, editor; Biner Design, designer; Juliette Peters, set designer; Jo Miller, photo researcher;
   Scott Thoms, photo editor

Photo Credits:
Capstone Press/Karon Dubke, cover (foreground), 8–9, 10, 18 (both), 21
Comstock Images, cover (background)
Corbis/Erik Freeland, 1; zefa/D. Attia, 11
Getty Images Inc./Erlanson Productions, 14
The Image Works/Chet Gordon, 15
PhotoEdit Inc./David Young-Wolff, 17; Myrleen Ferguson Cate, 6
Photo Researchers, Inc./Dr. P. Marazzi, 5
SuperStock/age fotostock, 12–13
© 6/5/05 Union Leader Corp./Bob LaPree, 20

1 2 3 4 5 6 11 10 09 08 07 06

Table of Contents

Signs of a Food Allergy

Your lips suddenly begin to tingle and swell. Itchy red spots appear on your skin. Your throat feels like it's closing up. It's getting hard to breathe and your stomach hurts. What could be causing this? You may have an **allergy** to a food.

Fact!

An allergic reaction to food usually happens within two hours of eating the food.

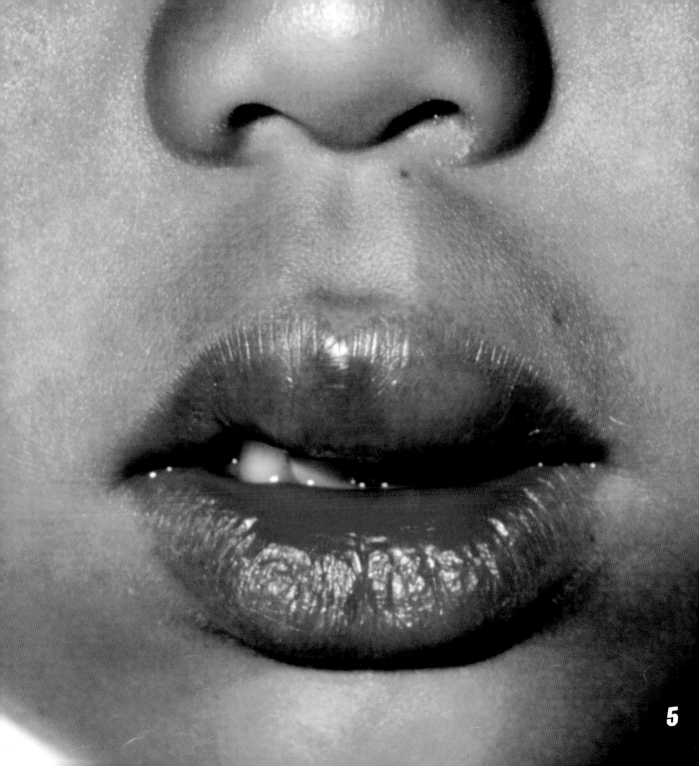

5

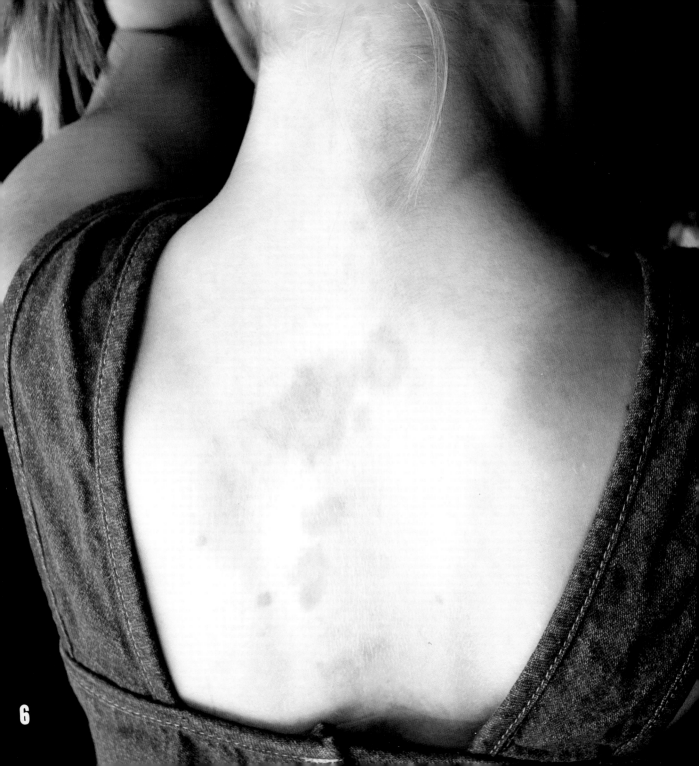

What Are Food Allergies?

Our bodies make **antibodies** to protect us from harmful germs. For some people, eating or touching certain foods sets off antibodies. Their bodies act as if the food is harmful. They start to have itching, swelling, or pain. This is an allergic reaction to food, or food allergy.

Fact!
The most common foods that cause food allergies are peanuts, tree nuts, fish, shellfish, milk, eggs, soy, and wheat.

How Do Kids Get Food Allergies?

Kids cannot catch allergies from other people. Scientists think that people who have food allergies are born with them. Food allergies sometimes run in families.

9

What Else Could It Be?

Not all reactions to foods are allergies. Spicy foods can make the mouth hurt. Other foods can cause harmless **rashes** around the mouth.

Some people have trouble **digesting** certain foods, like milk or bread. Eating these foods causes stomach pain. This is not a true food allergy.

Should Kids See a Doctor?

You should see a doctor if you think you have a food allergy. A doctor can test you for food allergies by scratching your skin with tiny amounts of foods. If the skin swells, you are allergic to that food. A blood test is another way to test for food allergies.

Treating an Allergic Reaction

A mild allergic reaction may not need treatment. Kids can take medicine that helps stop mild itching or swelling.

People with serious food allergies carry a shot of a stronger medicine. They use it if they have trouble breathing. Then they call an ambulance.

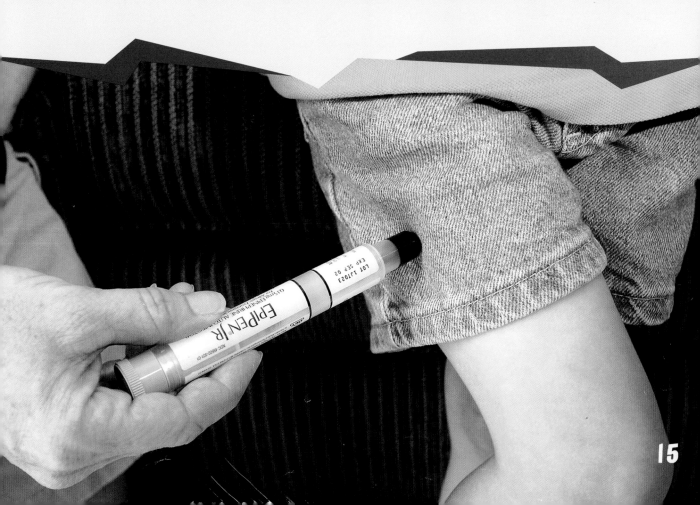

What Happens Without Treatment

Mild reactions usually go away in a few hours. But a mild reaction can turn into a more serious one. An allergic person who is having trouble breathing could even die if not treated right away. So people should always be watched carefully during an allergic reaction.

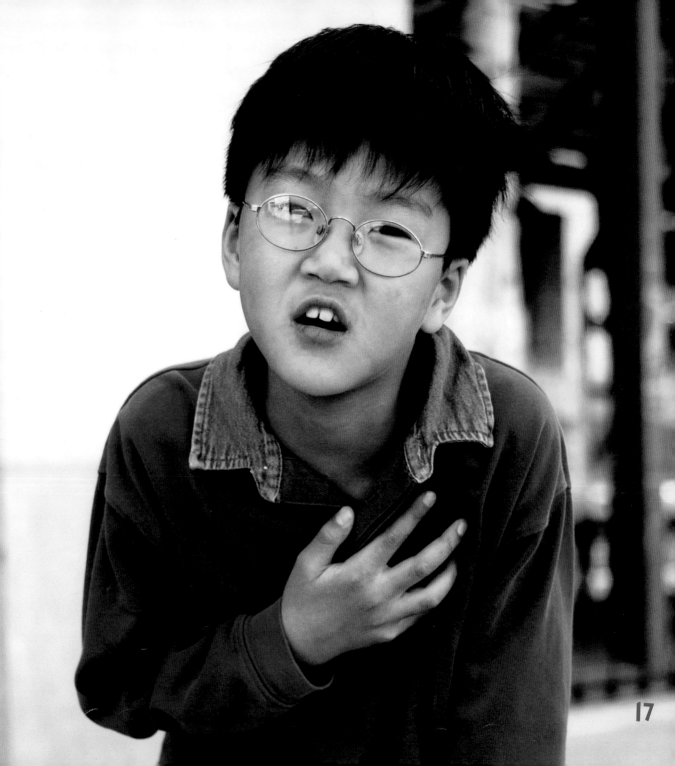

Per serving: Calories ~~~~~~~~~~~~~~, Total Fat 5g (8% DV), Sat. F~~~~~~~ ~~%
DV), Trans Fat 0g, Cholest. 0mg (0% DV), Sodium 65mg (3% DV), Total Carb.
~~~~~~

INGREDIENTS: GRANOLA (OATS, COCONUT [SULFITE TREATED TO PRESERVE COLOR], BROWN SUGAR, PALM KERNEL AND SOYBEAN OILS, CORN SYRUP, HONEY, SOY LECITHIN, SALT, PEANUTS, ALMONDS, EGG WHITES), CORN SYRUP, CRISP RICE (RICE FLOUR, SUGAR, WHEY, SALT, MALT [MALTED BARLEY FLOUR, WHEAT FLOUR, DEXTROSE]), PALM KERNEL AND SOYBEAN OILS, WATER, SORBITOL, NONFAT DRY MILK. CONTAINS 2% OR LESS OF EACH OF THE FOLLOWING: SOY LECITHIN (EMULSIFIER), SALT, CARRAGEENAN, SUGAR.

ALLERGY INFORMATION: CONTAINS SOY, PEANUTS, ALMONDS, EGGS, WHEAT AND MILK. MANUFACTURED ON EQUIPMENT THAT PROCESSES PRODUCTS CONTAINING PEANUTS AND TREE NUTS. M-206-14-S

Staying Healthy

There is no cure for food allergies. But kids can prevent reactions by avoiding the foods that make them sick.

Always read food labels to look for foods that aren't safe for you. If you have a serious food allergy, always carry your medicine with you.

Fact!
About 3 million children in the United States live with food allergies.

Amazing but True!

An allergy to peanuts can be one of the most serious food allergies. Some kids are so allergic that they can't even be near someone eating peanuts. They may react from breathing in tiny bits of peanut dust in the air. Some schools have "peanut-free" lunch tables to keep these kids safe.

Hands On:
Chocolate Cake

Many desserts are unsafe for kids with food allergies. Milk, eggs, and nuts, for example, are often found in cookies and cakes. Try this recipe for chocolate cake. It has no milk, eggs, or nuts. It's fun to see that you can make a delicious treat even without using these common ingredients.

What You Need

1 $1/2$ cups (360 mL) of flour
3 tablespoons (45 mL) of
  cocoa powder
1 cup (240 mL) of sugar
1 teaspoon (5 mL) of baking soda
$1/2$ teaspoon (2.5 mL) of salt
1 tablespoon (15 mL) of vinegar

5 tablespoons (75 mL) of oil
1 teaspoon (5 mL) of vanilla
1 cup (240 mL) of water
2 mixing bowls
spoon
tube pan

What You Do

1. Preheat the oven to 350°F (180°C).
2. Combine dry ingredients in a mixing bowl and mix well.
3. Mix wet ingredients together in a separate bowl.
4. Add wet ingredients to dry ingredients and mix until you get a smooth batter. Do not beat.
5. Pour into greased and floured tube pan.
6. Have an adult help you put the cake into the oven. Bake for about 35 minutes.

21

Glossary

allergy (AL-er-jee)—reaction to something that is harmless to most people, such as food, pets, or dust

antibodies (AN-ti-bod-ees)—substances in the body that fight against infection and disease

digest (dye-JEST)—to break down food so that it can be absorbed by the body

rash (RASH)—an area of skin that becomes red, itchy, or irritated

Read More

Gordon, Sharon. *Allergies.* Rookie Read-About Health. New York: Children's Press, 2003.

Rogers, Robyn. *No Lobster, Please! A Story of a Child with a Severe Seafood Allergy.* Boston: Heartsome Publishing, 2003.

Royston, Angela. *Allergies.* It's Not Catching. Chicago: Heinemann Library, 2004.

Internet Sites

FactHound offers a safe, fun way to find Internet sites related to this book. All of the sites on FactHound have been researched by our staff.

Here's how:

1. Visit *www.facthound.com*

2. Choose your grade level.

3. Type in this book ID 0736863915 for age-appropriate sites. You may also browse subjects by clicking on letters, or by clicking on pictures and words.

4. Click on the **Fetch It** button.

FactHound will fetch the best sites for you!

Index